Leaving Present

Jamie Doughty

This book is for Harriet

To Amy
We are
outside
the cider
house
Jam i℃x

CONTENTS

ACKNOWLEDGMENTS

First and foremost thanks to Sally Do for being the best. Thanks to all of my family and friends who have supported me all along. I would also like to thank everyone I have worked with over the years and everyone I might work with in the future. There is still time, after all the way things are going we are never going to retire.

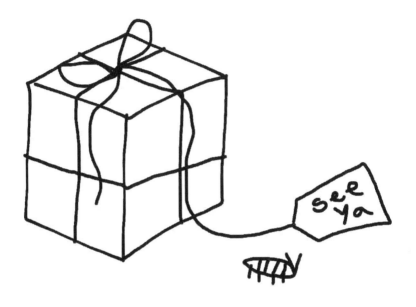

Seagulls Number 2

The seagull took a dump on the lid of my takeaway tea
As I took a drag on a roll up
Pointed out this fact to another smoker
He was concerned where this bird had come from
And potentially how much radiation was in that squit
I removed the lid from the cardboard cup
And finished the hot juicy tea
And proceeded to the job interview
Removing my jacket as I entered the building
As the seagulls muck
Had also splashed onto my sleeve

The Lid Has Flipped

The lid has flipped
This wasn't in the script
Should have been another Monday
I think they call it a blip
Villain in a comic strip
Point the finger at the guilty party
Tuckers lucky like Todd Carty
Rather unfortunate twisted fire starter moment
All buckled and bent
Foot nearly went through it
No malicious intent
Ambitions of being a gent
Dashed in a second
Dunderhead
You're not Ted Dibiase
Just a little bit bossy
Remember not to cross me
Had to switch from coffee to tea
Difficult to adjust to a new routine
This scene depicts a mean has-been
With A bad head should have took codeine
Green around the gills
Popping more pills
To pay more bills
Too many one nil's
We need to make this easier
How can I make it sound any cheesier?

On The Bus

So there's these two girls sat on the bus
And they're moaning about just about everything
This old guy sat behind them interjects
And they respond with
"Just but out and mind your own business"
And he says
"I couldn't help over hearing"
And one of the girls replies
"We are having a private conversation
Shut up and clean your teeth"
The old guy says
"You should have more respect for your elders"
And the response is
"I got loads of respect for the elderly I work in a residential home
thank you very much"
At this point I had a plan to say to the old guy
"Respect for the elders?
You should have more respect for yourself!
Cos these two bitches really aren't worth talking to"
But I just rang the bell
And got off the bus

LEAVING PRESENT

Browsers

Saw a t shirt I liked the look of
Took it off the rail
Held it up in front of the mirror
After looking at the extremely reasonable price tag
Decided I was going to buy it
Took a few seconds to ponder this though
And as I did
A trendy young couple
Are admiring the same t shirt
The blokes taken it off the rail
He's going to buy it
His girlfriend approves
But then they glance at me
And realise
That this balding 35 year pot bellied man
Has made the same choice
They put the shirt back on the rail
And leave the store

Worst Job

Someone got caught short
Someone got caught short
Someone got caught short by the back door
Someone got caught short

It was a fairground worker
It was a fairground worker
It was a fairground worker
Who got caught short by the back door

It was your boss who saw
It was your boss who saw
It was your boss who saw the fairground worker
Had left something at the back door

He got you to pick it up
He got you to pick it up
He got you to pick up a fairground workers poo
At the backdoor

Happy Days

Happy days!
Not again
What did you say?
What did you do?
Your lungs hurt
You didn't sleep so well
You are full of dread
As you walk down each corridor
You feel terrified of the prospect of what is around the next corner
You find yourself in a situation where you have to talk to someone
You're completely vacuous
And uncomfortable
You see if you had put all those hours gaming, drinking and generally vegging
Into something more constructive
You might find yourself where you want to be
So where do you want to be?
On the sofa with a can and a controller?
You've reached your dream destination
Happy days
Until the next heavy night

Duck Coincidence

Warped door
Water on the floor
Enter the text editor
Hear the dinosaur roar
Furthermore I got biscuits on the table
Totally unable to peel off the label
Re-cable the chicken wire electric fence
Substantial defense around the circumference
Noisy cups and ping pong balls drink Slupsk
Duck mans got more ducks on the corner
Store many things under the wing
Bring it all with you
In the evening
Back at the office
Using ordinary vocabulary
Monetary value is not even necessary
Eye on the timer
Never a high climber
I'm-er getting stuck so I'll just shut up

The Ghost of a Woodlouse

Went to the bathroom
Took a seat on the throne
And that's when it appeared
The ghost of a woodlouse
It's crawling along the cold tiles
And then it vanishes
These things happen
Think nothing of it
A week later the apparition returns
Does the walk across the room
I'm being haunted by the ghost of a woodlouse
The boogie bug
I know why
At the age of two I took that woodlouse
Alive and kicking
Between my thumb and forefinger
And shoved it in my mouth
And sucked the life out of it
My mother tried to save it
But when I eventually released it from my jaws
It was too late
The body of the woodlouse lay colourless
And covered in dribble
Thirty three years later
The ghost of the woodlouse
Is appearing in front of me
It's got hair
And eyes

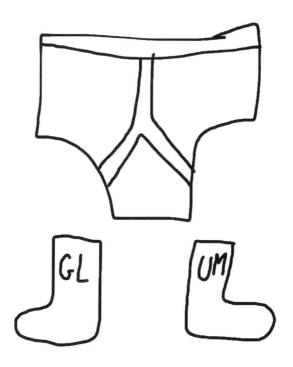

Glum

Spending the day like that was pretty lonely
Took the bus to town and exchanged pleasantries
with cashiers
Small town bloke making small talk in the big city
Fed up so he uses his return ticket
Roll another and smoke it
Deodorant deodorant deodorant
Looking forward to the evening
Deodorant deodorant deodorant deodorant
Passing by complete strangers
Invisible by day, wait till later
Cold meat no bread
Disguised as previous incarnation
Doing nothing, earning something
No direction no direction
Push buttons for no one
Neither fast nor slow
Running late for nothing
Blue socks blue pants
Watch another film
Fall asleep before the end
Roll another and smoke it
Deodorant deodorant deodorant
Looking forward to the evening
Deodorant deodorant deodorant deodorant
Passing by complete strangers
Invisible by day, wait till later
Cold meat no bread
Disguised as previous incarnation

Leaving Present

It was his last day
He was moving on to bigger and better things
Yeah he felt good
He didn't expect a leaving present

LEAVING PRESENT

The staff are on pretty low pay here
And everyone loathed him
He gave two of his favourite members of staff £20
And told them to go to the nearest HMV
So they could pick up the latest ministry of sound   compilation
A leaving present to himself
It was great to get a bit of time off
Going down HMV to do a bit of shopping
They found what the boss wanted
It was £16.99
They put it back on the shelf
And continued browsing
In the sale section
They found some yodeling compilations
And "The best horror film theme music in the world Vol.2"
And an exercise DVD featuring Timmy Mallet
And some badges featuring the cast members of Glee
The total cost of these hilarious items was £20
It was a no brainer
He'd see the funny side
Back at the shop
The manager was looking forward to hearing his new tunes
He can see the assistants with the HMV bag
Good lads. He knew he could trust them
Smirking they presented him with the bag
"What the fuck have you done with my £20?
Where the fuck is my cd?
Fucking yodelling
Fucking glee
What the fuck do you pricks think you're playing at?"
"We thought you would see the funny side"
"Have you got the receipt?"
  "Go and change it for ministry of sound you clowns!"

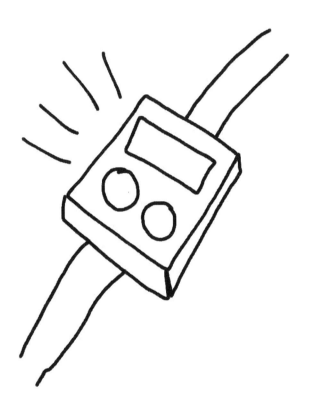

LEAVING PRESENT

Mike Knight

When I was a lad
I had no interest in open mic night
I used to have a dream
I wanted to be mike knight
I had a grey jogging suit
That had a picture of mike knight on it
It also had a picture of KITT
A copy of look in ran a special offer
If you sent them six pounds
They would send you a replica
Of Mike Knights digital watch
The one he used to talk to KITT on
Started saving for it
But on 50p pocket money a week
It was going to take some time
About six weeks later
I was halfway there
The second week of October
Let's go to the fair
Hook a duck
Dodgem cars
Helter Skelter
And then as if by magic
Three one pound notes appeared in a puddle
Stick them in your pocket
And don't tell no one
Go home and fill out the coupon
Sort out the postal order
Wait 28 days for delivery
Mike knights replica timepiece
A lone crusader in a dangerous world
With an hourly chime
And a stopwatch

UP ↑
DOWN ↓
LEFT ←
RIGHT →
A + START

New Game

Got some spending money
Going down town
Get down to the game shop
To purchase a new game
There's a couple of new ones out
Not sure what to buy
The helpful staff
Will be able to inform the final choice
FIFA or Tiger Woods
FIFA or Tiger Woods
FIFA or Tiger Woods
FIFA or Tiger Woods
Well
If you want a football game
Get FIFA
If you want a golf game
Get Tiger Woods
If you want a football game
Get FIFA
If you want a golf game
Get Tiger Woods
If you want a football game
Get FIFA
If you want a golf game
Get Tiger Woods
If you want a football game
Get FIFA
If you want a golf game
Get Tiger Woods
If you want a football game
Get FIFA
If you want a golf game
Get Tiger Woods

Shake a Bucket

Shake a bucket
Shake a bucket
Shake a bucket
All day long
Shake a bucket
Shake a bucket
Shake a bucket
All day long
Shake a bucket
Shake a bucket
Shake a bucket
All day long
I might give you some change
But if you jump up and down
And ask me how it's going
With a clipboard in your hand I won't
No offence
Carry on
I hope you hit your target
I'm going this way
To look for something to do

A Dog Could do That

A dog could do that
A dog could do that
A piece of canvas and a paint splat
A dog could do that

A dog could do this
A dog could do this
Write and read and rhyme the word "this" with "this"
A dog could do this

I wish I was your dog
I wish I was your dog
Your dog has more creative juice than the average person
Oh I wish I was your dog

Dull

I had a teacher who showed us
Different types of weather
Using laminated flashcards
Each card was cut into two parts
One a picture and one a word
We took it in turns to match a word to an image
One of the illustrations
Didn't have a matching word
We struggled to work out
Which type of weather was on display
The picture showed a boy frowning
Take a look in his eyes
Total despair
He was looking out of the window
Everything outside was brown and orange
A tree stood bare

LEAVING PRESENT

And the sky looked grey
The teacher seemed to take great pleasure
In informing us
This weather is dull
This weather is dull
This weather is dull
This weather is dull
I'm not sure I agree with this
Yes I love the sunshine
But I've always questioned her description
I have never seen a dull icon
On a weather map
Dull? Dull? Dull? Dull?
Maybe the boy in the picture had realised
That his life was a bit dull
He wanted to be outside but instead
He had to stay in with little to keep him entertained
Apart from a copy of Whizzer and Chips
That he had read 50 times cover to cover
And one Star Wars figure
It's true he could watch the television
But he finds it dull
He finds the music on the radio is dull
The food in the cupboards is dull
The local paper that was just delivered is dull
And so he decides to keep looking outside
Contemplating the rest of his dull existence
His time at school was dull
He got a job that was dull
The town he lived in was dull
The shows on the tv are dull
The music on the radio is dull
The book he is reading is dull
And this is all getting a bit dull

Fitting In

It wasn't a good idea to go to that club
You knew that when they told you to tuck
Your t-shirt into your jeans
The doorman might think this looks smarter
But his waist isn't 28 inches
It was around this time
It became apparent

LEAVING PRESENT

That those kind of places
Were never going to be your cup of tea
That's not to say you haven't had any fun
Somewhere like that
It's just that you felt happier
In a different kind of environment
Not really a problem is it
Or should I say was it?
The present day presents us with
A much more frightening concept
Tonight you could be singled out
Because you just don't look right
It's something that cannot be avoided
But the same goes for the event
That you have been looking forward to
For a few days
I must be getting on a bit
I'm going to advise you
Not to do what I did
It cost me quite a few quid
I can still see what the glass did
And I felt like a complete bastard
And that's it
Don't play that place another visit
Well done
What do you want a biscuit?
You're persistent
I'll give you that battle-axe
Just present us with the facts
And we'll be off your backs
And this is where I start to backtrack
With a bit of luck
We'll have better weather
Next summer

Man with Wheelie Bag

There's a bloke with a wheelie bag
There's nothing in it
He pushes it everywhere
He shouts at the cars
And he shouts at the sky
People laugh as he walks by
They don't realise what he's really doing
Yes he's pushing a wheelie bag
Down the road
But have you got any idea where he goes
I know
It takes him 24 hours to walk the earths circumference
In a straight line
As the crow flies
Really don't know how he gets across water
All I know is we need this man
With a wheelie bag
With nothing in it
He's stopping wars
And predicting scores
And so much more than that
Go on ask him!
Anything!
He always knows the answer
He won't tell you what it is
He just shouts at the cars
And he shouts at the sky
But you know he knows

Squirreling Things

I'm like a squirrel
But I don't have red or grey hair or a big bushy tail
Not a cartoon character like secret squirrel
Not a computer game character like conker
I do like hanging out in the park

LEAVING PRESENT

But I'm not very good at climbing trees
However I am like a squirrel
You see the thing is that when I've left a load of stuff lying around
and my miss us asks me to tidy up
A load of receipts, flyers and magazines,
Dead batteries, maybe a crisp packet or something like that
I get it all together and stick it in a bag
And shove it under the bed
Or sometimes in a draw instead
A couple of months later she finds it and says
"You squirrel things"
I squirrel things
I squirrel things
I squirrel things
I squirrel things
I squirrel things
I'm like a squirrel
Nice one Cyril
I've always been the same
I like squirreling things
But there's a problem
One major drawback
It's when it comes to moving house
I have to go through every squirreled bag
Just in case it contains something important
In fact the more I think about it
The more apparent it becomes that I should stop
Squirreling things
Squirreling things
Squirreling things
Squirreling things
Squirreling things

Smiler

Alright smiler
What you smiling at?
I only met you 5 minutes ago
And you want to know all my business
For some reason I answer all your questions
Truthfully
Not sure how you did that smiler
I don't read magazines
When I'm on the bus
And I don't speak
I overheard you smiler
Talking about quiet people
You said that quiet people are boring
Not everyone wants a laugh and a joke smiler
Well not when they're feeling like crap
I overheard someone else smiler
When that lot that bitch about them
Were in the room
You wouldn't speak to them
But when they left
You fancied a chat
Naughty smiler

Team Talk

You think that you can't do another day
You think that you can't do another day
Sitting there sniveling
You can't face doing this
It really is that bad
Do you really think that's the way?
Just because you don't feel ok
Get up get up
I can think of so many people feeling anxious and paranoid
Do you think they carry on?
They don't have a choice
And those bastards that grind you down
Will be there 24/7
You can't switch them off after 8 hours
And after all this was your choice
To do this
And now you say you can't do another day
Get up get up get up
Did you get past the front door?
I hope you did
They could do with someone like you
And what you do is so much more worthwhile
Than being out there

JAMIE DOUGHTY

Wake up Call

Wake up wake up
Present you with a coffee cup
But it just isn't enough
Feeling too rough
Don't want to rise
We'd rather improvise
Than advertise
Products that are broken
Paid per the word that is spoken
No fun for anyone no joking
No point going outside
You'll get soaking
Hardly inspirational
Far from being sensational
This is everyday living
The gift that keeps on giving
Really should start acting normal
This chat will be informal
Until the next time
Pantomime horse
We got the resources
Feeling lazy
Hearing noises
Fill the kettle and switch it on
Gulp that drink and get gone

ABOUT THE AUTHOR

Part bloke, part squirrel.

Made in the USA
Charleston, SC
30 June 2011